First Part

Supplement to the Individual Celebration of the Sacrament of Penance

I
THE SACRAMENT OF PENANCE AND RECONCILIATION

I

(*Compendium of the Catechism of the Catholic Church*)

296. What is the name of this sacrament?

It is called the sacrament of Penance, the sacrament of Reconciliation, the sacrament of Forgiveness, the sacrament of Confession, and the sacrament of Conversion.

297. Why is there a sacrament of Reconciliation after Baptism?

Since the new life of grace received in Baptism does not abolish the weakness of human nature nor the inclination to sin (that is, *concupiscence*), Christ instituted this sacrament for the conversion of the baptized who have been separated from him by sin.

298. When did he institute this sacrament?

The risen Lord instituted this sacrament on the evening of Easter when he showed himself to his apostles and said to them, "Receive the Holy Spirit. If you forgive the sins of any, they are forgiven; if you retain the sins of any, they are retained" (John 20:22-23).

299. Do the baptized have need of conversion?

The call of Christ to conversion continues to resound in the lives of the baptized. Conversion is a continuing obligation for the whole Church. She is holy but includes sinners in her midst.

302. What are the essential elements of the sacrament of Reconciliation?

The essential elements are two: the acts of the penitent who comes to repentance through the action of the Holy Spirit, and the absolution of the priest who in the name of Christ grants forgiveness and determines the ways of making satisfaction.

304. Which sins must be confessed?

All grave sins not yet confessed, which a careful examination of conscience brings to mind, must be brought to the sacrament of Penance. The confession of serious sins is the only ordinary way to obtain forgiveness.

305. When is a person obliged to confess mortal sins?

Each of the faithful who has reached the age of discretion is bound to confess his or her mortal sins at least once a year and always before receiving Holy Communion.

309. Is a confessor bound to secrecy?

Given the delicacy and greatness of this ministry and the respect due to people every confessor, without any exception and under very severe penalties, is bound to maintain "the sacramental seal" which means absolute secrecy about the sins revealed to him in confession.

310. What are the effects of this sacrament?

The effects of the sacrament of Penance are: reconciliation with God and therefore the forgiveness of sins; reconciliation with the Church; recovery, if it has been lost, of the state of grace; remission of the eternal punishment merited by mortal sins, and remission, at least in part, of the temporal punishment which is the consequence of sin; peace, serenity of conscience and spiritual consolation; and an increase of spiritual strength for the struggle of Christian living.

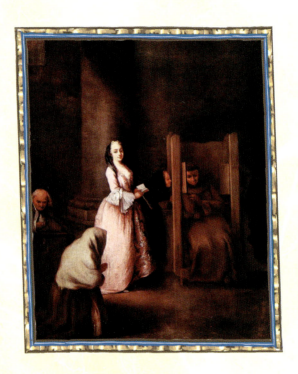

II
Preparation for Confession

Ephesians 2:4-10

Brothers and sisters: God, who is rich in mercy, because of the great love he had for us, even when we were dead in our transgressions, brought us to life with Christ—by grace you have been saved—, raised us up with him, and seated us in the heavens in Christ Jesus, that in the ages to come he might show the immeasurable riches of his grace in his kindness to us in Christ Jesus. For by grace you have been saved through faith, and this is not from you; it is the gift of God; it is not from works, so that no one may boast. For we are his handiwork, created in Christ Jesus for the good works that God has prepared in advance, that we should live in them.

To experience Reconciliation is something overwhelming: it literally means passing from death to life. You are invited to see yourself in this passage. The offer of salvation and complete happiness summons you to an audit of your life before Jesus. This passage from the Letter to the Ephesians gives you the chance to acknowledge with humility and courage your spiritual and existential situation. In which of these experiences do you recognize yourself right now?

1 **"God, who is rich in mercy, because of the great love he had for us, even when we were dead in our transgressions, brought us to life with Christ."**

I have never completely entrusted my life to another. I do not know well what it means to love and be loved. I am not satisfied with the life I am living. Where can I find what I need?

I am conscious of the contrast between Your bounty and my poverty, between Your all and my nothing. I do not consider myself worthy to be in Your presence (cf. Mt 8:8). I am not even sure that You will forgive me. There was a time when I followed Your teachings, but today I am very far from them. I feel that I need You, but I do not know what to do.

2 **"For by grace you have been saved through faith, and this is not from you; it is the gift of God."**

I love my freedom, and I do not relish the thought that my life is somebody else's work. Why should I have to account to anyone? But at times, alone or with others, I am assaulted by a strange sadness, and I am not successful at giving myself the full happiness that I seek. Lord, I need You to save my life.

3 **"God,...raised us up with [Christ],...that in the ages to come he might show the immeasurable riches of his grace in his kindness to us in Christ Jesus."**

The person of Christ stuns and fascinates me; He shakes my certainties. I am familiar with His words, and I consider Him a model of life, even if it is sometimes difficult to follow Him. But Christ does not propose Himself as an example to follow.

I

He wants to be the Lord of my life. He wants me to acknowledge Him as God. I have been told that He is the answer to every question that unsettles me, but I continue to resist. Is it really necessary to obey in order to be free?

4 **"For we are his handiwork, created in Christ Jesus for the good works that God has prepared in advance, that we should live in them."**

My life is not an accident. It is Someone's work. There is a plan for me. I understand that You ask me to do great things in order to follow You on Your way. I am not sure that I am capable of this. Your way passes also through the Cross. They have told me that true joy, the greatest grace, is to follow You along the way that You trod (cf. Pope Francis, *Homily at Saint Martha*, May 28, 2013). But I still have so many doubts, and I am afraid to go at Your pace.

A MORE THOROUGH EXAMINATION OF ONE'S PERSONAL SITUATION

1 **"God, who is rich in mercy, because of the great love he had for us, even when we were dead in our transgressions, brought us to life with Christ" (vv. 4-5a).**

I have already experienced the sadness of isolation: when I guard jealously my time and my energies I find myself more alone and sad. They have told me that life is meant to be given away, to be lived in communion with You and others. I understand it: death is total isolation, and every experience of isolation is a foretaste of the desolation of death. This also epitomizes my sin: disorder, disintegration, desert. I have consciously chosen it until it has become almost a habit, an entrenched interior inclination. At this point the reason does not much matter to me. Many live indulging every urge without concern: why shouldn't I do it? After all, I am not hurting anyone. Thus I live for today and let myself be carried away by habits, mine and those of others, almost without emotion, not even deriving pleasure from them.

I want an easy life. I want to enjoy the time I have without asking too many questions. I'm always on the lookout for novelties, new sources of excitement. I get bored quickly. And in my relationships, I am always ready to throw in the towel without a second thought. The feelings of the moment drive my decisions and promises: as soon as my feelings change, I find myself empty once more and without life goals. This too is an experience of death.

Actually, I know well that excuses and false myths only contribute to making me more miserable. If I were to explore the true reason for my anxiety I should ask myself to whom I am genuinely entrusting my life, in whom or in what I place my hopes for happiness. I need to give a meaning to who I am and to what I am experiencing. Insufficient for me is the happiness that depends on circumstances or moods, the freedom that obeys nothing and no one.

That truth is that without my earning it I am loved immensely by an eternal love. You give me the chance at fulfillment: You have granted me to live anew by taking my death upon Yourself. This awareness removes the obstacles that separate me from You. It is difficult to remain indifferent in the face of such love. "One cannot know Jesus without becoming involved with Him, without gambling one's life for Him" (Pope Francis, *Homily at Saint*

Martha, September 26, 2013). You ask me to trust You and to gamble on Your faithfulness, but I am not ready.

2 **"For by grace you have been saved through faith, and this is not from you; it is the gift of God" (vv. 5b, 8).**

It is not always easy to live according to Your Law; it is even less easy to accept being completely dependent on You. I give much of myself. I busy myself in the parish and in volunteer opportunities. I try to do my best at work and in the family. Why should I depend on You to be "good"? When I sin, the responsibility is mine; when I do well, it is Your gift; but then where is my freedom?

In my life there are tangible signs, facts that stir something in me; they open my eyes momentarily. There are great and pure desires. And this too is

not enough. I do not trust completely. I let myself make compromises. In times of temptation, I have asked myself if You are really interested in me. This is the crux of the matter, the first leap of faith, the most decisive: choosing to believe or not to believe that You love me, that You want to be involved in my life without robbing me of my freedom. The fear of not being loved is the root of every sin.

But one thing is clear to me: I cannot save myself. You do not impose upon me Your help; but when I think that I can do everything on my own, I find that I am weak. I believe that I know what is good, but I do not always manage to do it (cf. Rom 7:18-19). "This is our life: walking under grace, because the Lord has loved us, has saved us, has forgiven us. The Lord has done it all, and this is grace, the grace of God. We are on a journey under the grace of God...this opens up to us a vast horizon" (Pope Francis, *Diocesan Meeting of the City Vicariate,* 2013). Your grace does not take away my freedom: rather it throws open to it a horizon.

I

Salvation arrives as a surprise, sweeping away the plans and monotony of days all alike, and it does not necessarily fit my desires and expectations. It is a grace, Your free gift. But for this You do not despise the work of my hands. Faith is the first of Your gifts, but I am asked to receive it, guard it, and make it grow: it remains alive only if I deepen my encounter and friendship with You.

My very humanity testifies that what I do is not inconsequential: desires, aspirations, and abilities that You have given me want to be realized for the good. It is up to me to agree to the salvation that You have already offered me. On my own, I fall. If I hold on to You, I am buttressed in the struggles and temptations that present themselves every day. This is why it is so important to remain united to You by means of prayer and the Sacraments.

"I counsel you to remember the gifts you have received from God so that you can pass them on to others in turn. Learn to reread your personal history. Be conscious of the wonderful legacy passed on to you from previous generations (Benedict XVI, *Message for the 28th World Youth Day*, n. 2). If I gaze back carefully at my life's story, I become aware that it is punctuated by persons and experiences through which You have taken the first step to meet me. With this confession, I want to commit myself to reviving my gaze so as to recognize the signs of Your entry into my life. I want my examination of conscience to begin with an act of thanksgiving.

3 "God,...raised us up with [Christ],...that in the ages to come he might show the immeasurable riches of his grace in his kindness to us in Christ Jesus"(vv. 6a, 7).

"In Christ Jesus": Your generosity toward me is the mercy that is so great that it becomes Man. It is Jesus, who gives me life. I often have the arrogance to think that I know what I need: I measure and calculate the "level" of my involvement with You. I struggle to make space for You in my day, because I do not actually believe that You truly intervene in my life. Surely, You are present, but I am not always inclined to see You *tucked into the folds of my life and to understand that You can change my life. It is easy for me to reduce You to an empty or abstract thought unrelated to my life or to something to be taken for granted.* The veil that hides my life from my own eyes is removed in my meeting Your Son Jesus: my entire humanity is purified and transformed in Him.

"Being Christian is not the result of an ethical choice or a lofty idea, but the encounter with an event, a person, which gives life a new horizon and a decisive direction" (Benedict XVI, *Deus caritas est*, 1). My being Christian cannot be reduced to observing certain rules or belonging to a group or even embracing only what I consider "good for me." *To be Christian means to be Yours, even if I try to avoid it. I wind up in the same place as those who, listening to Jesus, refused to acknowledge him:* "Is he not the carpenter's son? Is not his mother named Mary and his brothers James, Joseph, Simon, and Judas?" (Mt 13:55). *This is an attempt to reduce Him to a known quantity that can no longer upset me very much.*

I

Who are You for me, Jesus? "I am the way and the truth and the life" (Jn 14:6): *this is Your claim.* It is difficult to remain faithful to this. These days it seems more "serious" and interesting not knowing where one is headed, living in a state of perpetual indecision and making no commitments. I know people who have chosen Your way to the end: they testify to me that following You is happiness. You are their Friend, the fullness of their joy. *When I meet a true friend, I feel alive again. It is a taste of Paradise. I want You, who make beautiful and complete all that I experience. It is the "hundred-fold" that You promised* (cf. Mt 19:29). I cannot cover up the encounter I have had, but distrust slows me down; Your face, real and present, however, provokes me to a response just as real.

4 **"For we are his handiwork, created in Christ Jesus for the good works that God has prepared in advance, that we should live in them" (v. 10).**

Lord, You know that I have spoken my "Yes" in freedom and for love of You. And yet I am often dissatisfied, despite all Your gifts. I continue to seek my fulfillment, my affirmation. It is not always easy to understand what You want from me. Sometimes I get lost in empty thoughts instead of desiring that "Your kingdom come, Your will be done" in my life. I am not as willing as I thought. I am afraid of losing myself.

A mild anxiety attends me, even regarding past decisions. At times, I am tempted to pull back: it has happened that I have defaulted on commitments or broken my word. Are You perhaps jealous that I am happy? I don't understand why I have to sacrifice myself when everything is going poorly, even if it is not my fault.

But You pass by and challenge me to respond to You. I am at a crossroads: I must realize why I was born, why I was created, whose I am. Many people invite me to avoid problems, to make due with a smooth life. Occasionally, it has seemed to me that I could live this way, but I emerged from this way of living more tired and weighed down. There are many indications in my life that I was made "to": to be truly myself, to be happy.

I have in my heart an impulse to the good; I want to give myself over to it. But it entails work, continual labor on my part. O Christ, not even You were able to get out from under the load of Your call. The grace of my call, of the meaning of my life, is not a possession gotten in one fell swoop.

"How can a person once grown old be born again?" (Jn 3:4). Many times I make Nicodemus's question my own. I find myself feeling old, a prisoner of the situations of my own making. In such times, I lose hope; I automatically close the door to the newness of life that You bring to me. Even Your dearest friends were tempted in this manner; to reduce You to what they themselves thought about You and to diminish thus also their vocation. "Do you also want to leave?" (Jn 6:67-68) From across the centuries, Your question reaches me and obliges me to answer: without You, I do not know where to go; my life remains a mystery to itself.

To those who follow You, You do not promise to take away their labors, but to lighten them, filling them with meaning. *"Take my yoke upon you and learn from me, for I am meek and humble of heart; and you will find rest for yourselves. For my yoke is easy, and my burden light"* (Mt 11:29-30).

Mysteriously, this is the way to my self-realization. At times I am afraid, I hide myself so as to

play loose with You. But when I take You serious-
ly, I am joyful. This is not the naïve optimism of
someone who thinks everything is easy; rather, it
is the fullness that comes from encountering You:
the recognition of Your voice that speaks continu-
ally in the circumstances of my life.

"We were created for good works": my days begin in goodness and are destined to goodness. It
is not always easy to remain faithful to my high
calling, but today You remind me that my life is the
answer to Your call. You are the guarantor of my
fidelity: "The one who began a good work in you
will continue to complete it until the day of Christ
Jesus" (Phil 1:6).

My activity, my doing, is *the continuation of*
a work that Another has begun; this is the root
of my hope. Today, to hope means to recognize in
all that happens to me Your plan of love, the plan
You devised for me when I was still being "*knit...in*
my mother's womb" (Ps 139:13). *Nothing of what I*
am is concealed from You. "*You probe me and you*
know me," *and You welcome me wholly as I am and*
want to bring everything to fulfillment. Only You
love me like this. Having perceived the extent of
Your love, I resist settling for anything less. "What
profit is there for one to gain the whole world and
forfeit his life?" (Mk 8:36).

SLOWING DOWN IN ORDER TO REFLECT

"Fixing his gaze on him, he loved him...."
Today, Jesus personally lingers with you and for
you. He loves you (cf. Lk 24:29). Before His coun-
tenance, daily preoccupations become reshuffled
and go in a different direction. You are not facing a
stranger, since in Him and through Him you were

wanted, created, and loved (cf. Eph 1:3-14). He knows you and loves you. This means that He sees something worthwhile in you, a friend. In whatever situation you find yourself, Jesus fixes His gaze on you to tell you that He loves you. "This is God's style: He is not impatient, as we are, we who frequently want everything immediately, even with people.

"God is patient with us because He loves us— the One who loves understands, hopes, trusts. He does not abandon or cut ties with us, but knows to forgive. Let us remember this in our Christian life: God waits for us always, even when we have withdrawn from Him! He is never far, and if we return to Him, He is ready to embrace us" (Pope Francis, *Homily on the Feast of Divine Mercy,* April 7, 2013).

At the root of our existence, at the root of the whole world, is not our heart's desire for happiness, but God, who desires and wants for us the fullness of life. Our search for happiness has already found its object. By sincerely and trustingly returning Jesus' gaze, you can draw on the fullness of life that you seek.

And if you do not find anything good in your life, ask yourself what robs you of hope? This is sin: all that separates you from God and from His friendship.

But fear not! Despite this, the Lord loves you. It was not you who looked for Him first, but He who chose you (cf. 1 Jn 4:10; Jn 15:16-17).

"Each of us, each one of us, is that little lost lamb, the coin that was mislaid; each one of us is that son who has squandered his freedom on false idols, illusions of happiness, and has lost everything. But God does not forget us, the Father never

I

abandons us. He is a patient father, always waiting for us! He respects our freedom, but He remains faithful forever. And when we come back to Him, He welcomes us like children into His house, for He never ceases, not for one instant, to wait for us with love. And His heart rejoices over every child who returns. He is celebrating because He is joy. God has this joy, when one of us sinners goes to Him and asks His forgiveness." (Pope Francis, *Angelus*, September 15, 2013).

Try to recall all the gifts that God has given you. Surely, they are many. Start out again from these signs of His love in order to rediscover the right balance.

Looking Within

What robs you of hope? What inside you keeps you from knowing love?

What are the obstacles to meeting the Lord? Perhaps lukewarmness, ignorance, your sexuality lived wrongly, your inability to sacrifice, to give up something for someone? What keeps you from leaving everything? The dread of missing out on happiness, or the feeling of shame, or the fear of disappointing your loved ones?

"Where God increases, man does not decrease: there man too increases and the world becomes luminous" (Benedict XVI, *Mass in the Sanctuary of Altötting,* September 11, 2006). You have received much; you cannot keep this gift for yourself (cf. Mt 10:8). You realize easily that what you do, whether good or evil, has an impact on those who are close to you. If you conduct yourself in an exemplary manner, someone will profit from your example. If you conduct yourself poorly, someone will pay on account of you and with you. There is a contamination that comes from our evil deeds and our silence. These create a heavy environment; they lead to disorientation and frightful imitation.

One should be able to have a different experience in the presence of a child of God—in school, in the workplace, at home, and in recreational activities. Being Christians is our life's adventure; it is more than right conduct according to the commandments. To be Christians is to belong to Christ, to have a living relationship with Christ, to be bound to God in a personal and profound way (cf. *Youcat*, n. 348).

Do you keep your relationship with Christ alive and active? Do you try to know Him always better, as a friend does with a friend? Are you familiar with the Word of God? Do you listen to it through the living and present witness of the Church?

If you love God, it makes no sense to use His name lightly or indeed with meanness, perhaps in a moment of "anger." To tell one's own name to another, to call and be called by name is a sign of great trust. God has let Himself be known by revealing to us His name, and by means of this name He has opened a way for us to approach Him, to recognize Him as present, to access His heart (cf. *Youcat*, n. 359).

If you have understood how good is that which the Lord asks of you, it makes no sense to deprive a Father of the joy of one day a week, Sunday, spent in His friendship. If you entrust yourself to Him, know that He is a jealous God (cf. Ex 34:14), and He expects that you will give Him all your faith, that you will place in Him all your hope, that

you will direct towards Him all the vigor of your love (cf. *Youcat*, n. 352). *Prayer is a non-negotiable facet of your relationship with God, which allows you to express yourself freely with Him and to welcome His free initiative of love in the circumstances in which you find yourself. Have you understood the value and beauty of daily prayer, of listening and praising, of adoring His presence and of putting forth your petitions?*

If you love your neighbor, you are concerned to respect your body so that you may make of it a gift full of love; your thoughts remain uncomplicated and your decisions are motivated by sincere love (cf. Rom 12:1-2). Love is the free gift of one's heart. It enables us to come out of ourselves and our selfishness. The love between a man and woman, conceived in the reciprocal and definitive gift that each one makes of himself or herself in marriage, becomes an image of God's communal love; it makes man similar to God. The virtue of chastity trains you to love like this; it enables you to have beautiful and solid relationships; it makes your actions expressions of a love that is faithful and trustworthy (cf. *Youcat*, nn. 402, 404).

Have you known how to deal with your energies and your friendships in order to follow through on an intention to love, without chasing after desire or the feelings of the moment? Have you known and experienced the beauty of chastity, which does not deny a part of you but orients it towards a total gift of the self in response to God's call? The Lord calls you not to conform yourself to the desires of the world, but to love the world with His heart (cf. Jn 15:12).

Are you welcoming? Do you train yourself in generosity? The one who is trustworthy in little, is trustworthy also in much; anyone who is dishonest (or avaricious) in small matters will be like this also in great matters (cf. Lk 16:10). How much of your time, your energies, and your material goods have you given away? Have you been able to laugh with those who were rejoicing and to suffer with those who weep? How have you spoken about others? Do you know that your words too can wound and kill?

What is your duty in the Church? To follow Jesus is to follow Him who is the Way, the Truth, and the Life. It is He who offers you the truth about yourself, the truth about man. How have you been faithful to Him? How have you been faithful to the truth that He gives you through His Word and the Church? With what sort of spirit have you rendered service in the context of the Church? Have you sought acclaim? Have you sought yourself rather than serve God's kingdom?

What witness have you provided in your civic responsibilities, in your duties (at school, work...), in your life in the midst of others? Are you concerned to be competent and to develop yourself, in order to bring through all that you are and do the Gospel into civic society? Do you cherish and keep communion in all you do with your relatives, friends, colleagues, and coworkers? Do you defend the dignity and the incomparable worth of every human being, from the moment of conception until the moment of natural death?

You have surely understood that a joy is greater when it is shared, that pain is tolerable when a loved one stands by you. Have you been able to be close to others? *You have been full of yourself, proud, disheartened* (cf. Rom 12:9-16).

Do you truly desire to encounter the Lord? Do you want to?

Come and see (cf. Jn 1:39).

MAKING A DECISION

"Fixing his gaze on him, he loved him...."

At this point I have two options: either I surrender to Your love and let myself be embraced (cf. Lk 15:20) or I leave sad and more lonely (cf. Mk 10:22).

Give me, Lord, the joy of letting myself be reconciled to You (cf. Jn 15:11).

I want to entrust my steps to Mary in humility and simplicity of heart. It was for this that her life so pleased You, and it is for this that You gave me Your Mother as my Mother.

My encounter with God's mercy has great value also for those who are close to me, because the newness of life that is given to me is a cause for joy, but not only for God. The Father calls all His heavenly friends to celebrate every son that returns to Him. Even the Church rejoices for me and with me. She thanks God and thanks me too for this celebration.

What **practical commitment**, verifiable and measurable, do you want to make, in order to live out faithfully this new encounter with God?

After the Sacrament of Reconciliation, try to **write down your commitment**, so that it may remain forever.

III
INDIVIDUAL CELEBRATION OF THE SACRAMENT OF PENANCE

I

RECEPTION OF THE PENITENT

When the penitent comes to confess his sins, the priest welcomes him warmly and greets him with kindness.

Then the penitent makes the sign of the cross which the priest may make also.

In the name of the Father, and of the Son, and of the Holy Spirit. Amen.

The priest invites the penitent to have trust in God, in these or similar words:

May God, who has enlightened every heart, help you to know your sins and trust in his mercy.

The penitent answers:

Amen.

READING OF THE WORD OF GOD (Optional)

CONFESSION OF SINS AND ACCEPTANCE OF SATISFACTION

Where it is the custom, the penitent says a general formula for confession (for example, I confess to almighty God) before he confesses his sins.

If necessary, the priest helps the penitent to make an integral confession and gives him suitable counsel. He urges him to be sorry for his faults, reminding him that through the sacrament of penance the Christian dies and rises with Christ and is thus renewed in the paschal mystery. The priest proposes an act of penance which the penitent accepts to make satisfaction for sin and to amend his life.

The priest should make sure that he adapts his counsel to the penitent's circumstances.

PRAYER OF THE PENITENT AND ABSOLUTION

The priest then asks the penitent to express his sorrow, which the penitent may do in these or similar words:

My God, / I am sorry for my sins with all my heart. / In choosing to do wrong / and failing to do good, / I have sinned against you / whom I should love above all things. / I firmly intend, with your help, / to do penance, / to sin no more, / and to avoid whatever leads me to sin. / Our Savior Jesus Christ / suffered and died for us. / In his name, my God, have mercy.

Then the priest extends his hands over the penitent's head (or at least extends his right hand) and says:

God, the Father of mercies, / through the death and resurrection of his Son / has reconciled the world to himself / and sent the Holy Spirit among us / for the forgiveness of sins; / through the ministry of the Church / may God give you pardon and peace, / and I absolve you from you sins / in the name of the Father, and of the Son, ✚ and of the Holy Spirit.

The penitent answers:

Amen.

PROCLAMATION OF PRAISE OF GOD AND DISMISSAL

After the absolution, the priest continues:

Give thanks to the Lord, for he is good.

The penitent concludes:

His mercy endures forever.

Then the priest dismisses the penitent who has been reconciled, saying:

The Lord has freed you from your sins. Go in peace.

IV
LIVING THE GRACE RECEIVED IN THE SACRAMENT OF RECONCILIATION

The Sacrament of Reconciliation is a privileged moment in which God grants His mercy. If man thought that he might be able to merit salvation by some means, every attempt to attain it would generate the frustration of never "doing enough" *(satis facere)* to merit such grace.

The relationship of God and man does not rest on a dynamic of expiation of one's own sins. The confession of sins, even if repeated many times, does not make us "worthy" of God's love, but opens us up to the awareness that the grace received sacramentally is the gift that transforms the heart and the way that leads to the forgiveness of sins. God awaits and welcomes the small steps of the one who returns to Him, and He does not demand perfection in order to grant His benevolence. This allows every person to surrender himself to the embrace of the Father and to begin again. The celebration of the Sacrament of Reconciliation does not make us "sinless," but strengthens our desire to respond to God's gracious love.

Life, renewed by the experience of the Sacrament, becomes for the believer the opportunity to give to others that which he has received from God. As happens in human relationships, in which the beloved desires to respond to the lover's goodness, the forgiven person experiences that the utter graciousness of the love received is a model and example of life. The one who has welcomed God's forgiveness and mercy realizes that he will have true peace only when he himself is successful in transmitting to others what he has been given. This was Jesus' teaching to the Eleven in the Cenacle: I have given you an example, so that you also may do as I have done (cf. Jn 13:15).

The case of Zacchaeus's conversion, who changes his life radically and repays more than the law demands, shows that from the heart of the forgiven man come forth profound sentiments that alter his manner of life and orient him towards a following of Jesus that is inspired by the good news (cf. Lk 19:1-10). The one who has experienced grace will feel the need to reconstitute —gradually or completely—his personal relationships, in order to offer and to receive forgiveness from his brothers and sisters.

From reconciliation there begins a journey of interior renewal that affects relationships and even the perception of the meaning of existence and the world. To squelch the desire for change, an authentic movement of the heart inspired by the Holy Spirit, would be to refuse the gift of grace that transforms a man's life and sentiments. After confession, therefore, it is necessary to give expression to the impulse of love that pervades the soul and to respond to the Lord by loving in a new way the brothers and sisters who are nearby, reshuffling the priorities of our life.

Welcoming the loving forgiveness of the Father moves the human person to come out of himself, out of the safe circle of affections and relationships, so that he may place himself at the service of his brothers and sisters who are tested by poverty, misery, illness, and pain. A greater sensitivity develops

I

for the other person's suffering, and love becomes the response to the grace received because grace tailors one's deeds and attitudes to the actions of Christ Jesus (cf. Eph 5:1-2).

Because sin ruptures fraternal communion, this Sacrament also reconciles the penitent with the ecclesial community. The gift of the Spirit, that through Christ the Father bestows on all His children, imparts the vitality to create a deep communion on the way to perfect unity (cf. Jn 17:11, 23). This impulse towards unity is expressed in the Eucharistic Prayer of the Holy Mass in which we ask "that, partaking of the Body and Blood of Christ, we may be gathered into one by the Holy Spirit." The Eucharist is the feast of forgiven sinners who gather together in order to become again one thing only in Christ Jesus.

The ecclesial community becomes the privileged place in which communion is safeguarded and experienced, realizing and making present what is narrated in Acts 2:42-47. The Church is the maternal womb in which the Word is heard, the Father is besought in unity, and the Eucharist is shared. It is not the place of the perfect, but those who are on the way to perfection; it is not the place of those who are already saints, but of those who by grace are clothed in the sanctity of God.

The Church is God's tent in the midst of His people, to whom the Lord Jesus assures His presence and His merciful love. Thus, reconciliation culminates in a rediscovery of one's parish, the dwelling of God's presence in the midst of His people, in which the assembly celebrates the mysteries of salvation throughout the liturgical year, awaiting the arrival of the glorious day when our Savior, Jesus Christ shall sit on the throne of His glory (cf. Mt 25:31-46).

SECOND PART
PERSONAL TESTIMONIES OF CONVERSION

Christians are called to permanent conversion, to a continual return to the merciful Father who waits with open arms for the prodigal son. To some of us there is given also the grace of a special conversion, an intense and exciting experience of God who touches and instantly changes the heart of those who are far away from Him.

Surprised at the conversion of Cornelius, Saint Peter says: "In truth, I see that God shows no partiality. Rather, in every nation whoever fears him and acts uprightly is acceptable to him" (Acts 10:34-35). Then he turns to his fellow Jews, scandalized by the conversion of the pagans, who were considered unworthy of the Lord's grace, and he adds: "Can anyone withhold the water for baptizing these people, who have received the holy Spirit even as we have?" (Acts 10:47).

Offered here are three personal testimonies in which the great gift of conversion comes into full view. As the Apostle Peter, we too thank God that He does not show partiality. The experience of conversion helps us to reflect upon and question how we are living out our return to God.

CONVERSION OF EDITH STEIN

(*Saint Teresa Benedicta of the Cross*)

II

We bow down before the testimony of the life and death of Edith Stein, an outstanding daughter of Israel and at the same time a daughter of the Carmelite Order (the words spoken by St. John Paul II on the occasion of the beatification of Edith Stein in Cologne on May 1, 1987).

Edith Stein was born on October 12, 1891, as the last child of eleven in a Jewish family of Breslau. Her memoires paint the portrait of a happy and religious family.

*The boys studied religion under the guidance of a Jewish teacher; they learned even a bit of Hebrew.... They learned the commandments, read passages from the scriptures, and they learned by heart some psalms (in German). They were always taught to respect every religion and never to speak ill of any. Grandfather taught his children the prescribed prayers. On Saturday afternoon, both parents called together the children who were at home to pray with them the afternoon and evening prayers and to explain them to them. The daily study of the Scriptures and the Talmud—an obligation for every Jewish man in the past and still the practice of Eastern Jews in the present—*was no longer observed in my grandparents' home. Yet all the prescriptions of the Law were observed strictly* (Edith Stein, *Storia di una famiglia ebrea*, Città Nuova, Roma 1998, p. 28).

At the age of 12, she met with the death of her father. This loss drastically affected family life.

Above all, the solemnity of the feasts was spoiled by the fact that only my mother and the younger children participated with devotion. My brothers, whose duty it was to recite the prayers in our father's stead, did so with little respect. If my elder brother was not present and the younger one had to take on the role of the head of the house, he let it be clearly known that interiorly he took this most lightly (Edith Stein, *Storia di una famiglia ebrea*, Città Nuova, Roma 1998, p. 78).

As a young woman she denied the faith and even became an atheist: *fully aware and by my own choice, I even gave up the habit of prayer* (Edith Stein, *Storia di una famiglia ebrea*, Città Nuova, Roma 1998, p. 16).

Observing the religious experience of Catholics entering St. Bartholomew's Cathedral in Frankfurt to pray there, she wrote:

It seemed strange to me. People entered the synagogues and Protestant churches I had visited only during the divine service. Seeing people come in between tasks, as a routine affair or for a spontaneous conversation, I was so struck that I could not forget the scene (A. Sicari, *Ritratti di Santi*, Jaca Book, Milano 1996, p. 148).

Then there began a gradual return to religious thought that ended with a sudden conversion in the summer of 1921, when Edith took in hand the autobiography of Saint Teresa of Avila.

Without choosing, I took the first book that I happened upon with my hand. It was a large volume entitled "Life of St. Teresa of Avila," written by herself. I began reading, and I was so taken by it that I did not stop until I got to the end. When I closed the book, I had to confess: "This is the truth" (Teresa Renata dello Spirito Santo, *Edith Stein*, Brescia 1959, p. 130).

On January 1, 1922, Edith Stein was baptized and so entered subsequently into the Carmelite monastery in Cologne, taking the name Teresa Benedicta of the Cross. Her life was brutally interrupted by the Second World War. She was killed in Auschwitz on August 9, 1944.

CONVERSION OF ANDRÉ FROSSARD

These words make one shiver: they are too full of conviction not to be convincing; they are too true to be denied, because they have been confirmed by a long life of unswerving and wholehearted faith (Card. Angelo Comastri concerning the testimony of conversion of André Frossard).

I worked hard in order to make a name for myself as a journalist and writer and thus to hope not be taken for a madman when discharging my debt: recounting what happened to me (André Frossard a Vittorio Messori in: Vittorio Messori, *Inchiesta sul cristianesimo*, Oscar Mondadori, 2010).

André was born on January 14, 1915, in a family in which religion was not even mentioned.

God did not exist. His image, the images that evoked his existence or that of what might be considered his progeny in history, the saints and prophets and biblical heroes, had absolutely no place in our house. No one spoke of Him to us. [...] We were atheists of the perfect kind, those who no longer question themselves about their atheism. The last anticlerical militants who lashed out against religion in public meetings seemed to us rather pathetic and somewhat ridiculous, as historians would have seemed who might undertake to disprove the fable of Little Red Riding Hood (A. Frossard, *Dio esiste e io l'ho incontrato*, Sei, Torino 1969, pp. 27, 30).

In the world marked by the total lack of reference to the Absolute, there was something that would not leave the young André tranquilly alone.

On my fifteenth birthday, finding at hand a bank note, I thought it suitable to my dignity to spend the evening with one of those kinds of ladies; and I took the Metro to Montparnasse [a place unfortunately well known for the presence of prostitutes]. Upon arrival, at the end of a long deserted corridor I ran into an emaciated beggar, who seemed as though he had been painted using black tar on a white ceramic wall, like the paintings of Matisse in the Chapel of Venice.

When the moment came for me to go past him, I felt that that evening I would not go further. Whether it was the pity or the stark contrast between that wretch reduced to stretching out his hand into the empty air and that which I was secretly and ashamedly preparing myself to do, whether it was the desire to carry out an unforeseen deed or the cowardly desire to put off an experience beyond my courage, I do not know; the fact is that the bills held in my fist at the bottom of my pocket went from there straight into that poor soul's cap, and I went back (to the Metro) to have my return ticket punched (A. Frossard, *Dio esiste e io l'ho incontrato*, Sei, Torino 1969, pp. 105-106).

II

Without prior warning, on a completely normal day, while waiting for a friend, André Frossard meets God or, better said, God meets him: God enters his life.

It is July 8. A magnificent summer. Directly in front of me, the rue d'Ulm opens wide its sunny trench all the way to the Pantheon [...]. My thoughts? I do not recall [...]. My interior state? Perfect, insofar as conscience may say: that is, without any of those anxieties that predispose to mysticism. [...]. Ultimately, I do not experience the least curiosity about those matters of religion that I maintain belong to a prior age. It is five thirty o'clock. In two minutes, I shall be Christian (A. Frossard, *Dio esiste e io l'ho incontrato*, Sei, Torino 1969, pp. 136-138).

Tired of waiting for his friend, he goes into the church nearby; he surveys the architecture and looks at the people who pray there.

At first, these words come to me: "Spiritual Life." They are not said, and they are not even formulated by me, but they are heard as if pronounced softly next to me by a person who sees what I do not yet see. The last syllable of this whispered prelude barely reaches the surface of my consciousness when suddenly a reverse avalanche begins. I do not say that the sky opens. It does not open. It thrusts itself. It rises suddenly, a silent thunderbolt, from that unsuspecting chapel in which it was mysteriously enclosed.

How can I describe it with these poor words that refuse to give me their help and threaten to intercept my thoughts to transfer them into the realm of the fantastic? How would the painter, to whom it were given to catch a glimpse of unknown colors, paint them? An indestructible crystal, of infinite transparency, of an unbearable luminosity (one degree higher would have done me in) and rather blue, a world, another world of such splendor and density that send our world in a flash into the fragile shadows of unfulfilled dreams. This world "is reality, the truth": I see it from the dark bank on which I am yet detained.

There is an order to the universe; and at the summit, beyond this veil of resplendent fog, the evidence of God, the evidence made presence, and the evidence made the Person whom a moment before I would have denied, the One whom Christians call "Our Father," whose entire sweetness I sense, a sweetness different from all others, which is not that passive quality that often goes by this name, but a sweetness that is active, shocking, beyond every force, able to smash the hardest rock and that which is harder than rock, the human heart.

Its overflowing and complete irruption is accompanied by a joy that is nothing other than *the exultation of the saved, the joy of the sinking person rescued just in the nick of time; however, with a difference, for it is in the very moment that I am being snatched up to salvation that I become aware of the mud in which I was immersed, without knowing it, and that I ask, seeing myself still half-submerged, how I could have ever lived and breathed there.*

II

At the same time, I am given a new family, the Church, that is charged with leading me where I must go—it being understood that despite appearances I must still traverse a certain distance, which can only be eliminated by the reversal of gravity.

These feelings that I strain to translate into the inadequate language of ideas and images are simultaneous, some comprised in others; and after so many years I have not yet exhausted their contents. All is overtaken by a presence, beyond and through an immense gathering, of Him whose name I may no longer write without trepidation of wounding His tenderness, Him before whom I have the fortune of being a forgiven son who awakes to learn that all is gift (A. Frossard, *Dio esiste e io l'ho incontrato*, Sei, Torino 1969, pp. 143-145).

When he exits the church, his friend, seeing that something has happened, asks him: What's happening to you?—*"I am Catholic," and, as if afraid of not being explicit enough, he adds: "apostolic and Roman"* (A. Frossard, *Dio esiste e io l'ho incontrato*, Sei, Torino 1969, p. 146).

André Frossard, Catholic journalist at the service of the Truth and the Church, died on February 2, 1995.

CONVERSION OF JOHN PRIDMORE

"I tell you, in just the same way there will be more joy in heaven over one sinner who repents than over ninety-nine righteous people who have no need of repentance" (Lk 15:7).

My name is John Pridmore. I was born in the East End of London, England. At the age of 10 my parents asked me to choose who I wanted to live with, as they were getting divorced. I think that this led me to the decision not to love again, as the people you love just crush you. At the age of 27, I had everything that the world believes are important for happiness: a penthouse flat, sports cars, and more money than I could spend. I had obtained my money through organized crime and making major drug deals. I was also involved in protection rackets and violence of all kinds. I used to have a long leather jacket with a sewn-in pocket in which I carried a machete. I tell you this not to glory in the past but in the Glory of God.

II

I arrived home on one typical night and became aware of a voice speaking to me inside my heart. I knew this voice to be God. At that exact moment, I said my first prayer and my life began to change.

Unbeknownst to me, my mum had been praying a novena to Saint Jude and it was on the last day of the novena that I had heard the voice of God.

This led me to go on a retreat, which was anything but what I thought it was going to be. The first talk was on a wounded heart. The priest said that each sin we commit is like a wound on our heart. As he spoke, I looked at a crucifix and I realized that Jesus had died for me so that my sins could be forgiven.

After the talk, I said a prayer to Our Blessed Mother Mary and asked her: "What does Jesus want me to do?" It was then that I heard her say: "Go to Confession." I was truly afraid of what the priest might think, but Mary gave me the courage and so I went to Confession.

For over one hour, I was completely honest with the priest and left nothing out. Then the priest placed his hand on my head and gave me absolution. But it was not his hand, it was Christ's hand. I knew in my heart that I was forgiven.

You see, I had never realized that our hearts are like a glass window, which on the one side is God's unconditional love pouring down every minute of every day, while on the other is all of our sins. In the end, we can become blind to how much God loves us and just see how unworthy of Him we are. I took all of that sin and tipped it out at the foot of the Cross and, I was alive again. I could feel the wind on my face. I could hear the birds singing as those sins had killed me inside. However, the Sacrament had brought me back to life. When I looked in the priest's eyes, I saw he was crying. He was not judging me. He was Jesus to me.

Now I live and work full-time for Jesus in St. Patrick's community based in Ireland. Many times I am asked by people as to how they are to have a personal encounter with Jesus Christ. I always say that by making an honest Confession is what allows Christ to come to us in the humility of this wonderful Sacrament of healing.

I now run parish missions around the world. At a mission in Derry, Northern Ireland, a man in his 80s came up to me to thank me. He went on to say that he had been going to Mass every Sunday since he was 7, but tonight he had met Jesus personally for the first time in 48 years after having gone to Confession.

During another mission, a 15-year-old girl said, "When you came to my school this morning, I did not believe in God. However, because of what you said I came tonight and went to Confession. Not only do I now know Jesus is real, but I know He loves me." She went on to say how Confession had changed her life.

The Sacrament of Confession has also changed my life. I thank Jesus every day for the wonder of His mercy. I now go regularly and each time I feel like I am made new again in His love.

II

THIRD PART
OUTLINE FOR THE CATECHESIS

The confession of sins has a long history, as long as mankind itself. In the very first experience of human transgression of the divine law, we see how sin drives Adam and Eve to conceal themselves. For the first time in human history we find God who in the Garden of Eden goes in search of man, asking: Where are you? (Cf. Gen 3:9.) It is an experience common to us all, that of seeking to hide our sins. On the other side, we have the liberating experience of confessing our sins. "If we acknowledge our sins, he is faithful and just and will forgive our sins and cleanse us from every wrongdoing" (1 Jn 1:9).

We cite here some texts that can move our hearts to confess our sins and to experience God's forgiveness in the Sacrament of Reconciliation.

III
The Saints and the Sacrament of Penance

The offender does not fear the severity of the judge: the goodness of Him who listens to him reassures him as he makes his confession.

—Saint Augustine, *Discourse 29/B*

III

To do penance is to bewail the evil we have done, and to do no evil to bewail.

—Pope St. Gregory the Great,
Forty Homilies on the Gospels

Confession is like a bridle that keeps the soul which reflects on it from committing sin, but anything left unconfessed we continue to do without fear as if in the dark.

—St. John Climacus,
The Ladder of Divine Ascent

Therefore it is evident that after sin the Sacrament of Penance is necessary for salvation, even as bodily medicine after man has contracted a dangerous disease.

—St. Thomas Aquinas, *Summa Theologica*

Strive always to confess your sins with a deep knowledge of your own wretchedness and with clarity and purity.

—St. John of the Cross, *Degrees of Perfection*

Go to your confessor; open your heart to him; enable him to see clearly all the recesses of your soul, follow the counsels which he gives you with great simplicity and humility; for God, who dearly loves obedience, often makes those counsels profitable which we take from others, and especially from directors of our souls, [...].

—St. Francis de Sales,
Introduction to the Devout Life

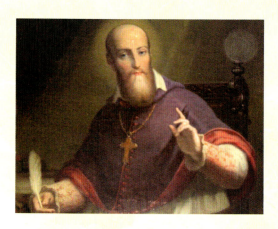

A soul does not benefit from the Sacrament of Confession if it is not humble. Pride keeps it in darkness. The soul neither knows how, nor is it willing, to probe with precision the depths of its own misery. It puts on a mask and avoids everything that might bring it recovery.

—Saint Faustina, *Diary*

Confession is an act of honesty and courage—an act of entrusting ourselves, beyond sin, to the mercy of a loving and forgiving God.

—Pope St. John Paul II, *Mass for the Faithful of San Antonio,* 1987

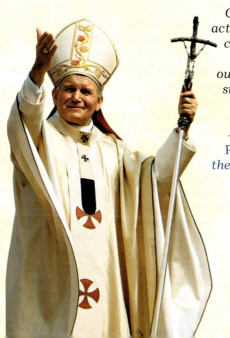

Catechesis of
Pope Francis
on the Sacrament of Penance and Reconciliation

General Audience, Wednesday, February 19, 2014

The Sacrament of Reconciliation is a Sacrament of healing. When I go to confession, it is in order to be healed, to heal my soul, to heal my heart and to be healed of some wrongdoing. The biblical icon which best depicts forgiveness and healing in their deep bond is the episode of the forgiveness and healing of the paralytic, where the Lord Jesus is revealed as the physician of souls and bodies simultaneously (cf. Mk 2:1-12; Mt 9:1-8; Lk 5:17-26).

1 The Sacrament of Penance and Reconciliation flows directly from the Paschal Mystery. In fact, on the evening of Easter the Lord appeared to the disciples, who were locked in the Cenacle; and after addressing them with the greeting, "Peace be with you." He breathed on them and said, "Receive the holy Spirit. Whose sins you forgive are forgiven them, and whose sins you retain are retained" (Jn 20:21, 22-23). This passage reveals to us the profound dynamism contained in this Sacrament.

First, the forgiveness of our sins is not something we can give ourselves. I cannot say, "I forgive my sins." Forgiveness is asked for; it is asked of another; and in Confession we ask it of Jesus. Forgiveness is not the fruit of our own efforts but a gift; it is a gift of the Holy Spirit who fills us with the wellspring of mercy and grace that flows

III

unceasingly from the open heart of the Crucified and Risen Christ.

Secondly, it reminds us that we can truly be at peace only if we allow ourselves to be reconciled, in the Lord Jesus, with the Father and with the brothers and sisters. And we have all felt this in our hearts, when we go to confession with our soul weighed down and some sadness; and when we receive Jesus' forgiveness, we are at peace, with that peace of a soul that is so beautiful and that only Jesus can give, only He.

2 Over time, the celebration of this Sacrament has passed from a public form—because at first it was done publicly—to a personal one, to the confidential form of Confession. But this must not entail the loss of the ecclesial matrix which constitutes its vital context. In fact, the Christian community is the place where the Spirit is made present, the Spirit who renews hearts in the love of God and makes all the brothers and sisters one

thing in Christ Jesus. This is why it is not enough to ask the Lord for forgiveness in one's own mind and heart, but why it is necessary humbly and trustingly to confess one's sins to a minister of the Church.

In the celebration of this Sacrament, the priest represents not only God but also the whole community that sees itself in the weakness of each of its members, that listens and is moved by his repentance, and that is reconciled with him, that cheers him up and accompanies him on the path of conversion and of human and Christian growth. One might say: "I confess only to God." Yes, you can say to God, "Forgive me," and tell Him your sins. But our sins are also committed against the brothers and sisters and against the Church. This is why it is necessary to ask pardon of the Church and of the brothers and sisters in the person of the priest.

"But Father, I am ashamed...." Shame is also good. It is healthy to feel a little shame, because being ashamed is salutary. In my country when a person feels no shame, we say that he is "shameless," a *"sinvergüenza."* But shame too does good, because it makes us more humble. And the priest receives this confession with love and tenderness and forgives us on God's behalf.

Also from a human point of view, in order to unburden oneself, it is good to talk with a brother or sister and tell the priest these things which are weighing so much on my heart. And one feels that one is unburdening oneself before God, with the Church, with his brother or sister.

Do not be afraid of Confession! When one is in line to go to Confession, one feels all these things, even shame, but then when one finishes Confession one leaves free, grand, beautiful, forgiven, candid, happy. This is the beauty of Confession!

I would like to ask you—but don't say it aloud, let everyone respond in his heart: when was the last time you made your confession? Everyone think about it.... Two days, two weeks, two years, twenty years, forty years? Everyone count; everyone say to himself, "When was the last time I went to confession?"And if much time has passed, do not let another day go by. Go, the priest will be good to you. Jesus is there, and Jesus is more benevolent than priests. Jesus receives you; he receives you with so much love. Be courageous and go to Confession!

3 Celebrating the Sacrament of Reconciliation means being enfolded in a warm embrace: it is the embrace of the Father's infinite mercy. Let us recall that beautiful, beautiful parable of the son who left his home with the money of his inheritance. He wasted all the money; and then, when he had nothing left, he decided to return home, not as a son but as a servant. His heart was filled with so much guilt and shame.The surprise came when he began to speak, to ask for forgiveness. His father did not let him speak, he embraced him, he kissed him, and he began to make merry.

But I am telling you: each time we go to Confession, God embraces us. God rejoices! Let us go forward on this road.

From the Homily of
Fr. Raniero Cantalamessa, O.F.M. Cap.
Preacher to the Pontifical Household

Basilica of Saint Peter, Good Friday, April 6, 2012

The good thief made a complete confession of sin; he says to his companion who insults Jesus,"Have you no fear of God, for you are subject to the same condemnation? And indeed, we have been condemned justly, for the sentence we received corresponds to our crimes, but this man has done nothing criminal"(Lk 23:40-41).

III

Here the good thief shows himself an excellent theologian. Only God in fact, if He suffers, suffers absolutely innocently; every other being who suffers should say, "I suffer justly," because even if he is not responsible for the action imputed to him, he is never altogether without fault. Only the pain of innocent children is similar to God's and because of this it is so mysterious and so sacred.

How many atrocious crimes in recent times have remained anonymous, how many unresolved cases exist! The good thief launches an appeal to those responsible: do like me, come out into the open, confess your fault; you also will experience the joy I had when I heard Jesus' word,"Today you will be with me in Paradise"(Lk 23:43). How many confessed offenders can confirm that it was also like this for them: that they passed from hell to heaven the day that they had the courage to repent and confess their fault. I have known some myself. The paradise promised is peace of conscience, the possibility of looking at oneself in the mirror or of looking at one's children without having to despise oneself.

Fourth Part

A Proposal of Lectio Divina

In his Apostolic Letter *Evangelii Gaudium,* Pope Francis spurs the Church on to an affective relationship and vital encounter with the Word of God.

And now let us seriously set ourselves to listening to God. His Word is for me today, now. "If today you hear His voice, do not harden your hearts.…" Let us listen!

1st Outline

THE WORD
Ephesians 2:4-10

The Word of God

...Is Heard

God, who is rich in mercy, because of the great love he had for us, even when we were dead in our transgressions, brought us to life with Christ (by grace you have been saved), raised us up with him, and seated us with him in the heavens in Christ Jesus, that in the ages to come he might show the immeasurable riches of his grace in his kindness to us in Christ Jesus. For by grace you have been saved through faith, and this is not from you; it is the gift of God; it is not from works, so no one may boast. For we are his handiwork, created in Christ Jesus for the good works that God has prepared in advance, that we should live in them.

IV

...Is Pondered

In the text of the Letter to the Ephesians, the Apostle recalls the mercy of the Father as the distinctive note of all God's action in history. Precisely because God is mercy, every single human event, inserted into the flow of history, receives a highly salvific meaning. The forgiveness that the believer needs, when sin characterizes the decisions of his life, becomes visible in the love that God offers, going beyond human limits and granting pardon and love at every instant. It is as if God gave "His eternal mercy" as a constant refrain for the life of man created by Him in His image and likeness, and the ecstatic believer could sing, "I will bless the Lord at all times" of my life and my history.

"Israel remembers the Lord's goodness. In this history, there are many dark valleys, journeys of difficulties and death; but Israel recalls that God was good, and it can survive in this dark valley, in this valley of death, because it remembers. It remembers the Lord's goodness and His power; His mercy applies always. And this is important also for us: to remember the Lord's goodness.

"Memory strongly sustains hope. Memory tells us: God exists; God is good; His mercy endures forever. And thus memory opens up, even in the darkest day or time, the way to the future. It is the light and star that guides us. We too have a memory of the goodness, of the merciful and eternal love of God. Israel's history is already a memory for us, too, of how God revealed Himself, how He created a people of His own. Then God became man, one of us: He lived with us; He suffered with us; He died for us. He abides with us in the Sacrament and in the Word. It is a history, a memory of God's goodness that assures us of His goodness: His love endures forever" (Benedict XVI, *Catechesis*, October 19, 2011).

...IS PRAYED

1 For a brief moment I abandoned you, / but with great tenderness I will take you back. / In an outburst of wrath, for a moment I hid my face from you; / But with enduring love I take pity on you, / says the LORD, your redeemer.

This is for me like the days of Noah, / when I swore that the waters of Noah / should never again deluge the earth; / So I have sworn not to be angry with you, / or to rebuke you. / Though the mountains leave their place and the hills be shaken, / My love shall never leave you / nor my covenant of peace be shaken, / says the LORD, who has mercy on you (Is 54:7-10).

IV

2 **From Psalm 136**
Give thanks to the LORD, for he is good,
    for his mercy endures forever;
Give thanks to the God of gods,
    for his mercy endures forever;
Give thanks to the Lord of lords,
    for his mercy endures forever; [...]
Who remembered us in our abjection,
    for his mercy endures forever;
Who freed us from our foes,
    for his mercy endures forever;
Who gives food to all flesh,
    for his mercy endures forever;
Give thanks to God of heaven,
    for his mercy endures forever.

3 O Jesus, eternal Truth, strengthen my feeble forces.
You, O Lord, can do all things.
I know that without You all my efforts are in vain.
O Jesus, do not hide from me, for I cannot live
without You.
Listen to the cry of my soul.
Your Mercy has not been exhausted, Lord, so have
pity on my misery.
Your Mercy surpasses the understanding of the
Angels and of people put together;
and although it may seem to me that You do not
hear me,
still I put my trust in the ocean of Your mercy,
and I know that my hope will not be disappointed.
O Jesus, Eternal Truth, our Life, I invoke and beg
Your Mercy.

(Passage taken from the *Diary* of Sister Faustina
Kowalska)

2nd Outline

THE WORD
Luke 7:36-50

The Word of God

...Is Heard

A Pharisee invited him to dine with him, and he entered the Pharisee's house and reclined at table. Now there was a sinful woman in the city who learned that he was at table in the house of the Pharisee. Bringing an alabaster flask of ointment, she stood behind him at his feet weeping and began to bathe his feet with her tears. Then she wiped them with her hair, kissed them, and anointed them with the ointment. When the Pharisee who had invited him saw this he said to himself, "If this man were a prophet, he would know who and what sort of woman this is who is touching him, that she is a sinner." Jesus said to him in reply, "Simon, I have something to say to you." "Tell me, teacher," he said. "Two people were in debt to a certain creditor; one owed five hundred days' wages and the other owed fifty. Since they were unable to repay the debt, he forgave it for both. Which of them will love him more?" Simon said in reply, "The one, I suppose, whose larger debt was forgiven." He said

IV

to him, "You have judged rightly." Then he turned to the woman and said to Simon, "Do you see this woman? When I entered your house, you did not give me water for my feet, but she has bathed them with her tears and wiped them with her hair. You did not give me a kiss, but she has not ceased kissing my feet since the time I entered. You did not anoint my head with oil, but she anointed my feet with ointment. So I tell you, her many sins have been forgiven; hence, she has shown great love. But the one to whom little is forgiven, loves little." He said to her, "Your sins are forgiven." The others at table said to themselves, "Who is this who even forgives sins?" But he said to the woman, "Your faith has saved you; go in peace."

...Is Pondered

The mercy that Jesus voices declares without doubt the goodness, the tenderness, and the love of God. In Jesus' addressing Himself to the sinful woman in the city where He was we understand and recognize that Jesus' approach discloses to us the maternal traits of God's love. In the Old Testament, God is a father to Israel, a father that loves also with the care and tenderness of a mother. The term in Jesus' language that we have translated as "mercy" intends to express tenderness, the tender part of the person. The Hebrew language reinforces the term, referring its significance to a mother's womb that is moved for her son. The text of Isaiah is particularly evocative and emblematic in these hours of intense celebration of God's mercy: "In a time of favor I answer you, / on the day of salvation I help you / ... Can a mother forget her infant, / be without tenderness for the child of her womb? / Even should she forget, / I will never forget you" (Is 49:8a, 15). In God's mercy is found all God's action on behalf of His creature.

In the liturgy the Church celebrates the love that forgives with these words: "Lord, holy Father, almighty and eternal God...being rich in mercy, you constantly offer pardon and call on sinners to trust in your forgiveness alone. Never did you turn away from us, and, though time and again we have broken your covenant, you have bound the human family to yourself through Jesus your Son, our Redeemer, with a new bond of love so tight that it can never be undone" (Preface of Eucharistic Prayer for Reconciliation I).

IV

Since genuine love does not exist without the lover taking responsibility for the beloved, the merciful love of the Father, in Jesus Christ, takes upon Himself human sin. Precisely because sin is the inability to love, and therefore in sin all is an expression of selfishness, God, who is good and great in love, forgiving sins, gives tangible proof of His love, bestowing mercy as an expression of that which He is. Praise of God for His mercy is the root of our prayer. In the book of Exodus, the revelation of God's name is accompanied by the attributes of His holy name. "The LORD, the LORD, a merciful and gracious God, slow to anger and rich in kindness and fidelity" (Ex 34:6).

The mercy that Jesus expresses is first of all that of looking deeply, as He does in the case of the woman in the house of Simon the Pharisee.

"Jesus enjoys the flowering of love. He sees the woman come forth from the accounting of giving and having, as if she had a kind of score to settle with Jesus, and pour herself out in spaces of freedom and creativity, to the point of incinerating by one single gesture an entire inheritance of calculations and miseries. Every human gesture done with the whole of our hearts brings us close to the absoluteness of God.

"Jesus looks past etiquette. A woman arrives; others see a sinner; he sees a lover: she has loved much. Love is worth more than sin. It is our identity. The mistake you made does not revoke the good you accomplished; it does not cancel it out. A head of grain matters more than all the weeds of the field. This God who enjoys perfume and caresses moves us deeply. He is not the great accountant of the cosmos, but an offer of sunshine, the chance at a profound, joyous, perfumed life that knows the sources of joy, of song, and of friendship. A single gesture of love, even wordless and without echo, is more useful to the world than the noisiest action, than the grandest feat. It is Jesus' total revolution, possible for all, possible every day" (Ermes Ronchi).

...Is Prayed

1 **From Psalm 103**

Bless the LORD, O my soul;
  and all my being, bless his holy name.
Bless the LORD, O my soul,
  and forget not all his benefits.
He pardons all your iniquities,
  he heals all your ills.
He redeems your life from destruction,
  he crowns you with kindness and compassion.
Merciful and gracious is the LORD,
  slow to anger and abounding in kindness....
Not according to our sins does he deal with us,
  nor does he requite us according to our crimes....
As a father has compassion on his children,
  so the LORD has compassion on those who fear him.
For he knows how we are formed,
  he remembers that we are dust....
But the kindness of the LORD is from eternity,
  to eternity to those who fear him.

2 **From Psalm 32**

Blessed is he whose fault is taken away,
  whose sin is covered.
Blessed the man to whom the LORD imputes not guilt,
  in whose spirit there is no guile....
...I acknowledged my sin to you,
  my guilt I covered not.
I said, "I will confess my faults to the LORD,"
  and you took away the guilt of my sin....

You are my shelter; from my distress you will
        preserve me;
        with glad cries of freedom you will ring me around
Be glad in the LORD and rejoice, you just,
exult, all you upright of heart.

3 Almighty and merciful God,
how wonderfully you created man
and still more wonderfully remade him.
You do not abandon the sinner,
but seek him out with a father's love.
You sent your Son into the world,
to destroy sin and death
by his passion,
and to restore life and joy
by his resurrection.
You sent the Holy Spirit into our hearts
to make us your children
and heirs of your kingdom.
You constantly renew our spirit
in the sacrament of your redeeming love,
freeing us from slavery to sin
and transforming us ever more closely
into the likeness of your beloved Son.
We thank you for the wonders of your mercy,
and with heart and hand and voice
we join with the whole Church
in a new song of praise:
Glory to you
through Christ
in the Holy Spirit,
now and forever.

(*Rite of Penance*, Prayer of Thanksgiving)